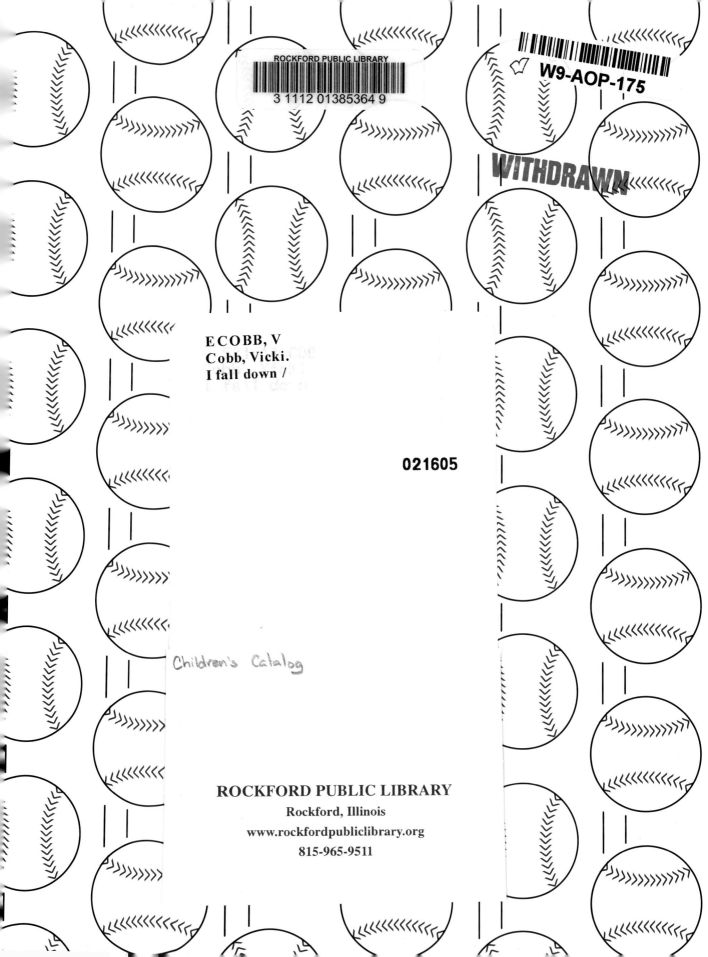

VICKI COBB
SCIENCE PLAY

I Fall Down

by Vicki Cobb
Illustrated by Julia Gorton

HarperCollins*Publishers*

For Jillian, Jonny, and Ben
—V.C.

This book is for you, Raleigh.
You fall down the most of anyone I know.
But you always get back up and try again
until you master yet another trick
on your skateboard.
—J.G.

The author gratefully acknowledges Dr. Dan Haas of the Eastman
Kodak Company and Dr. James C. Owens, service fellow, Torry
Pine Research, and member of the American Physical Society,
for their technical expertise. However, the author takes full
responsibility for the accuracy of the text.

I Fall Down
Text copyright © 2004 by Vicki Cobb
Illustrations copyright © 2004 by Julia Gorton
Manufactured in China by South
China Printing Company Ltd. All rights reserved.
www.harperchildrens.com

Typography by Julia Gorton
1   2   3   4   5   6   7   8   9   10
❖
First Edition

Note to the Reader

This book is designed so that your child can make discoveries. It poses a series of questions that can be answered by doing activities that temporarily take the child away from the book. The best way to use this book is to do the activities, without rushing, as they come up during your reading. You will have to help with some of the activities, such as tying shoelaces and dropping things into your child's hands. Turn the page to the next part of the text only after the child has made the discovery. That way, the book will reinforce what the child has found out through experience.

Before you begin reading this book to your child, have on hand an assortment of balls, keys, a block, a jar of molasses or honey, a spoon, a penny, a dry sponge, a small bar of soap, two identical rubber bands, a child's shoe, an adult shoe, and a bathroom scale. When you choose objects to drop, please use only solids with minimal air resistance rather than feathers or tissues.

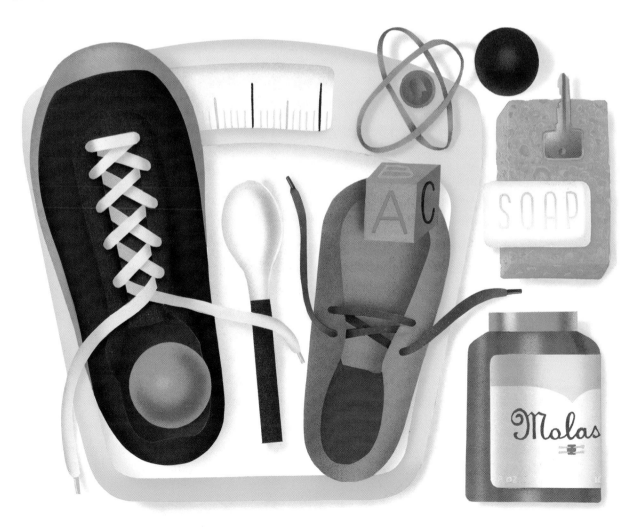

Know what happens when you trip?

You fall down!

Know what happens when you spill your milk?

It
drips
down
!

Throw a ball up into the air. Watch what happens. It goes up for a short time, then falls down.

Try tossing other things up in the air.

A block.

Your mom's keys.

When something falls, which way does it fall?

Does it ever fall up?

Know what makes things fall?

It's a force called gravity. As long as you are on earth, you can't get away from it.

Gravity is always pulling things.

Know which way? Down, down, down.

You can see how gravity pulls.

Take a spoonful of molasses or honey
and point the spoon down so that
the goo dribbles back into the jar.
Watch it drip!

The
goo
stretches
and gets
longer and
longer.
It looks
like a
ribbon
streaming
into the jar.
Gravity
pulls the
molasses
from
the
spoon
back
into
the jar.

Do some things fall faster than others?

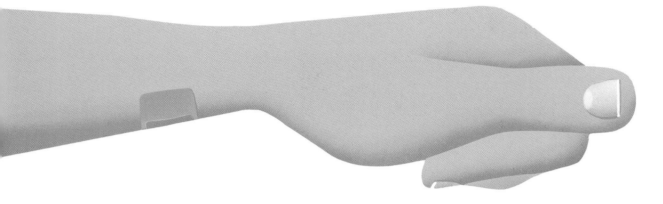

Try it and see!

Hold a penny and a key in one hand. Open your hand
so they both start falling at the same time.
Listen and watch as they hit the floor.

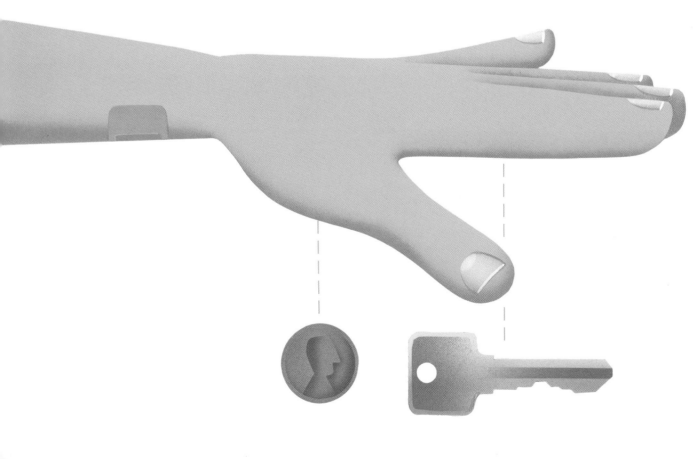

id either the penny or the key win the race, or was it a tie?

Have lots of

Things fall so fast
it's hard to tell
if there is a
winner or
a loser.

But no matter
whether the obje
are big or sma
it seems that
it's always a tie

mints

dropping races.

The only time
you have a
clear loser
is when you
drop something
that the wind
could easily
blow away,
such as a feather
or a tissue.
You see air
fighting gravity
only with very
light objects.

If there were
no air,
you would find
that gravity
pulls everything at
the same speed.

Astronauts proved this on the moon, where there is no air. Every dropping race was a tie.

AMAZING BUT TRUE!

Does everything land
with the same force?

Or do some things hit **harder** than others?

Here's a way to find out.

Have someone drop a dry sponge
into your hand from
about a foot above it.
Next try a small bar of soap.
Which hits your hand harder,
the sponge or the soap?

Try dropping lots of things into your hand.

Soon you will discover that some things hit harder than others.

Now hold the **bar of soap** in one hand

and the **sponge** in the other.

Which is heavier, the sponge or the soap?

Move your hands **up** and **down** to help feel the difference.

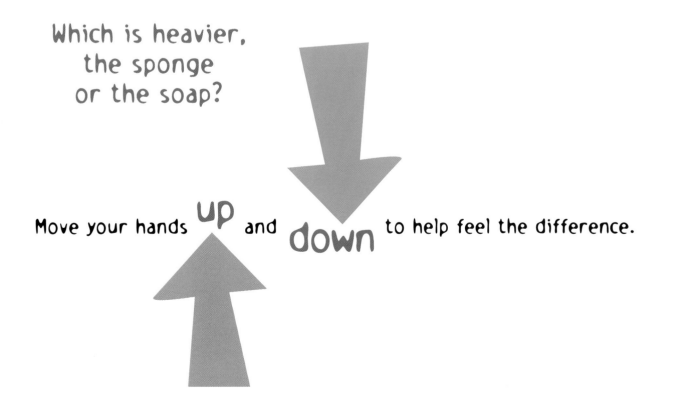

Your hands stop the SPONGE and

the SOAP from falling to the ground.

But you can still feel gravity's pull on the soap and sponge when you hold them in your hands. This pull is called weight.

You can see if one object is heavier than another without letting either of them fall. Here's how.

Get two rubber bands the same size.

Tie one
of your
shoes
to one
rubber
band.

Tie one
of your
parent's
shoes
to the
other
rubber
band.

Lift both shoes
by the rubber bands.
Which rubber band
stretches more?

The heavier shoe
stretches the
rubber band more.
Each rubber band acts
like a scale to
measure weight.

Your weight is a
measure of how hard
you fall when you fall down.

How much do you weigh?

74 62

39 98

45

50 85

How
much
does
your
mother
or
father
weigh
?

167

48 91 225

73

The more you weigh, the harder you fall.

But
you
don't
have
to
fall

in order to weigh yourself.

A scale
tells you
how hard
you fall—
without
you falling
at all!

So simply get on a scale.

Yay!